WITHDRAWN

GAMES CHRISTIANS PLAY

HARPER & ROW, PUBLISHERS
NEW YORK, EVANSTON, AND LONDON

GAMES
CHRISTIANS
PLAY

An Irreverent Guide to
Religion without Tears

By JUDI CULBERTSON and PATTI BARD

Drawings by SUSAN PERL

A portion of the material appearing in this book originally was published in somewhat different form in *Eternity* Magazine.

Contents

31406

PARAPHERNALIA

Preface

Anyone who has spent any part of his life sleeping in a pew knows there is more to being a Christian than meets the eye. Much more. There is the old, laborious, tried-and-true method of being kind to your neighbor, working like a dog, tithing, witnessing, living peaceably with all men, and so on. Fortunately, for those who are more impatient, there are certain shortcuts to becoming spiritual; that is, if you can *look* like a Christian, play the games right, you won't have to bother with all that other. And, in the time you save, you can get some *fun* out of life.

Here, then, is a beginner's handbook to Christian games, or how to live like the devil (though many settle for much less) and still be a saint.

GAMES CHRISTIANS PLAY

The Case of Mary Verily and Other Christian Tales

Mary Verily wanted to be spiritual. And she would have been, too, except for her husband. He was an atheist and flatly forbade her to darken the sanctuary door.

Sunday mornings, while he whistled "Hello, Dolly!" and set his Powerflow Lawnmaster roaring across the lawn, she would sit on her chaise on the terrace and sulk. "If it weren't for you," she would mutter bitterly beneath the roar of the lawnmower, "I could be a *real* Christian!"

"If it weren't for him," she would tell her sympathetic Christian friends, "I'd bake cakes for the covered-dish suppers!"

One day it happened. At first she couldn't believe it, but gradually, she accepted its reality: Her husband had been converted. And, worse, he wanted her to work in the church, to take her place beside him.

11

She found that she didn't want to at all. The prospect of standing up before anyone, of teaching or singing, made her break out in hives. As for that other kind of work (baking chocolate cupcakes and mending old sunbonnets), it was just a waste of time.

So she joined the church and learned to play I'D LOVE TO, BUT . . .

What Mary learned others may learn as easily: Everybody plays games. And Christian games aren't hard to learn at all. Christians have been playing games for at least a thousand years. Some authorities feel that they began with Adam when he tried a few rounds of IF IT WEREN'T FOR YOU directed not only at Eve, but at God Himself ("The woman whom *You* gave to be with me, *she* gave me of the tree and I did eat . . .").

You may be playing one or two games without knowing it. And even if you aren't, you will learn quickly.

You will learn, because Christians are a vigorous bunch, ready to pounce on new Christians with all kinds of demands and games that they have been playing for years. Their skill will make it impossible for you to look as if you are a radiant, winsome, friendly, hard-working Christian (RWFHC) when you are nothing of the sort. They will even make it hard for you to become a genuine RWFHC.

One game in particular blocks the way:

WHEN YOU HAVE BEEN A CHRISTIAN AS LONG AS I HAVE . . .

The players are the variety of Christian either born in the choir stall or who made decisions for Christ at age two-and-a-

12

half. No matter what your response is to them, these worthies will never let you forget that they were in the vineyard first.

If You Try Bible Study

You are enthusiastic—you'd say downright studious—when it comes to reading the Bible. You have purchased a commentary, a concordance, a dictionary of the Bible, a King James, a *New English Bible,* and a Revised Standard Version. The discoveries you're making are so exciting you want to share them. One day you do.

That's the day you hear, "Oh, well, it just doesn't seem possible you haven't heard of the taunt-songs addressed to the Chaldeans. I mean, don't you know *any*thing about the Book of Habakkuk? When you have been a Christian as long as *I* have . . ."

If You Try Christian Living

You feel strongly committed to a round of hospital visitation, cleaning the parish house, or giving to an Andean mission. You share your joy in giving with a Christian friend.

That's the day you hear, "Oh, well, I went through that stage myself when I was eleven. New Christians *love* to go overboard. But when you have been a Christian as long as *I* have . . ."

If You Don't Try Christian Living

No use trying to avoid being made the goat of this game. If, for instance, you have been "converted late" but are the type who is definitely not enthusiastic about Bible study, the sea-

14

soned laborer will sigh, "Oh, well, what can we expect? You have to be brought up with the Bible to appreciate it. In your case, the roots of sin have sunk so deeply that you cannot see the beauty of the Word of God, but when you have been a Christian as long as *I* have . . ."

The best ploy, of course, is to remain a cool goat.

Remaining a Cool Goat in Two Easy Steps

1. As soon as you have been a Christian for ten months, find yourself a likely-looking unbeliever and then set out to convert him. Time your evangelism so that he enters the fold when you have been a believer for a full year.

2. Shield him carefully from damaging contacts, making sure that he stays clear of people who have been Christians for two, ten, or forty years.

Then let him have it: "When you have been a Christian as long as *I* have . . ."

A second game, full of rewards for older Christians, is . . .

WELCOMING THE NEW CONVERT

Imagine yourself a new Christian. You have been seeing nothing but encouraging and nonpressuring faces, and may feel that this is one game you have been spared. Don't believe it. Don't make this mistake particularly if you are a woman, because many Christians feel that women have nothing important to do with their time anyway and can therefore be loaded down with coolie work.

15

Spotting the New-Convert Welcomer

You are automatically at a disadvantage in this game, because you are highly visible. Even if you are young and nicely dressed, it will be a shade too flamboyantly. Or expensively. Or at any rate *differently*. It could be just *those earrings*. As the new convert being approached, you should be on the watch for the bosomy, determined, motherly types on the one hand, or the dowdy, friendly, energetic *types* on the other. If someone is watching *you*, you have been spotted by a New-Convert Welcomer. Next comes . . .

The Attack

You feel a pressure on your elbow, and in your ear comes the cheerful sound of welcome. "You have no idea how happy we are to have you! And your lovely family. I've *already* signed you up as a nursery helper!" She will chuckle, knowing that you are still rather defenseless. "And—let's see—our missionary guild meets Thursday afternoons. I've asked them especially to put you in my circle."

"Oh, that's awfully nice of you but . . ."

"We take turns bringing refreshments and have a sociable time. And if we don't finish the handiwork, we just take it home with us and do it. You sing—don't you?" The implication is that anyone who *doesn't* sing falls somewhere between a social leper and a retarded ape.

"Well *yes,* but . . ."

"Now don't be bashful! Nobody is bashful around here. A busy Christian is a happy Christian. Remember the story of the cleaned-up house and the seven devils."

While you are trying to remember the story and decide

16

whether you are supposed to represent the house or the seven devils or both, she is signing your name on a piece of paper. It pledges you to make robes for the junior choir.

Defending Yourself against Other Christians

Now perhaps you find yourself the goat of this game, too. Is there anything you can do? Yes. There are several defensive Christian games, starting with Mary Verily's simple but effective ploy . . .

I'D LOVE TO, BUT . . .

The Importance of Being Prepared

It may happen any time, day or night, depending on how desperate the situation is. You hear the doorbell ring. It is the pastor, looking for men to do door-to-door canvassing. Or Mrs. Johnson, rounding up Vacation Bible School helpers. It is vital for you to have at least one good reason why it is impossible to do anything they might suggest.

To stand there and stammer "Why, I-I-" is to give them the opportunity to answer "Oh, fine! I *knew* we could count on you." Any refusal after that only creates ill will and defeats your larger purpose.

Employing Your Perfect Excuse

Think how much better it is to say immediately, "Oh, I'd love to, but I have seven small children under four . . ."

Or: "My pet ocelot died and we're holding a memorial service . . ."

18

Or: "My invalid aunt lives with me, and she's afraid of the dark . . ."

"Oh, that's a shame."

"Maybe next time. *Do* try me."

But after this happens once or twice, whenever your name is mentioned, someone will automatically mumble, "Can't . . . dead ocelot . . . afraid of the dark," and pass to the next name.

More specific assaults on your leisure can be repelled by a defensive game suited to many uses:

MRS. PEABODY'S CHURCH-KITCHEN GAMBIT

Unmolding the Jello

You are trapped in the kitchen during a fellowship dinner. Outside, a happy din rises. Inside, you toil among a bedlam of dirty platters, half-eaten rolls, and mountains of greasy plates. (No one ever finishes Mrs. Schneïder's applesauce-cabbage.) You are unmolding a jello salad for the dessert course while Mrs. Peabody, a sharp-eyed matron gameplayer, hovers over you, waiting to carry the jello out to the table—and disappear into the crowd.

Leaving you to scrape food, and wash dishes for the next four hours.

The male version of the entrapment is played

When It's Time for Spring Cleaning

The men of the church have begun their annual cleanup of the grounds. As a loyal member, you have been painting the edge of the downspout for several hours. Finally, out of black paint and beginning to arouse a few black looks, you head

toward the iced-tea table to take a break—only to find yourself behind the lawnmower, pulling the rope to get the thing started. This is extremely dangerous, as you may find yourself behind it for the rest of the day.

How to Escape

Fumble about clumsily. Debark a piece of the prize hemlock. Gouge the jello into a sticky ruin. It will soon be obvious to everyone that you are going to make a mess of it. Remain intent and try your hardest. Is it your fault if you fail? Then turn to the person nearest you, preferably *Mr.* Peabody, and say humbly, "You'd better do it, you know more about it." Stand and watch admiringly as he continues with great skill the job you have begun.

At the first opportunity, slip away!

As a last resort, consider . . .

I DON'T KNOW WHY THEY DON'T
DO SOMETHING ABOUT . . .

This is a nice way to shift the responsibility, to be on the giving side of the blame without anyone ever noticing that you are doing nothing about it yourself.

The Ubiquitous "They"

Obviously, "They" are the ones who should be doing something about the snow on the church steps, the pigeons in the belfry, the poor attendance at the women's society, the noisy children in the vestibule before the service.

Watch for your opening, then turn seriously to the person

beside you. "*I* think it's a disgrace! I don't know *why* they don't do something about it!"

Since it's not up to you, you are perfectly free to criticize it. And, if something *is* done, you can always be cantankerous and play, WELL, NOBODY BOTHERED TO ASK *ME* ABOUT IT.

Using Your Church to the Best Advantage

The people beside you in church on a Sunday morning are not merely people. They are also potential customers. It is on this assumption that the ancient game of SALESMAN is based. Building on this assumption, the successful player of SALESMAN chooses a product and sticks to it with the zeal of a Christian in the catacombs, until everyone in his church owns at least one.

Choosing Your Product

There are three categories, useful in narrowing your choice:

1. *Standard Brands:*   Girl Scout cookies, Christmas cards, Avon products, magazine subscriptions, jewelry, peanut candy, etc.

2. *Christian Brands:* Inspirational books, Christian recordings, textual notepaper, Christian greeting cards, plaster mottos, Bible storybooks, etc.

3. *Home-made Christian Brands:* Potholders, paperweights, faces carved from acorns, cereal boxes decorated with wrapping paper and stickers, plaques made from popsicle sticks, aprons, or anything else made by a Christian in less fortunate circumstances than you.

Should you be a cemetery-plot or insurance salesman with any ambition at all, you have already contacted everyone around you. Several times. A month.

Your Display Case and Sales Talk

Necessary equipment includes a case full of samples of your product, catalogues, order blanks, and in certain instances handkerchiefs and heart-rending photographs.

Naturally, you should cultivate a winning, persistent manner, a positive outlook, spiritual smile, and at least a basic understanding of guilt manipulation. Remember you should never be ashamed of playing SALESMAN. After all, aren't we all in the business of "selling" Christianity? Anyway, you should never be ashamed.

Approaching a Prospect

Waggle a finger or wink an eye until you've got his attention and:

"Look!" Whip out your sample case and throw it open. "Can you believe these gorgeous shell pins were made by an old, half-blind Cherokee, a dear Christian gentleman from Pahokee, Florida?"

"Really?"

"Yes. You can *see* how beautifully and delicately worked they are!" Hold out one done in gold with two comic eyes on it, and a larger cluster painted red and green, with "Silent Night" inked across the ribbing.

"Um—very nice."

"And such a dear Christian saint. So independent, in spite of everything. Won't take charity; insists on earning his own way."

"Oh."

Pause. Smile deprecatingly.

"Well, I guess I could take one. Certainly. Uh—how much are they?"

"Only two dollars apiece. How many will you need?"

Games to Make Sure You Win No Matter What

The most irritating thing in the world, after you have taken the trouble to worm your way into the fellowship of a church, is to find that there are people there who not only do not appreciate all you have sacrificed, but who have the audacity to criticize you. There is no reason at all why the people in any congregation cannot learn the Christian art of giving in gracefully; but once in a while, when you have trouble pointing this out to them gently, you will need to use force.

A really skillful player will be able to avoid most unpleasantness.

The easiest game to start with is . . .

PRIMA DONNA

Determining Your Eligibility

To play PRIMA DONNA you must have some irreplaceable talent, or at least the ability to convince people that you do. If you are planning to donate $20,000 for the new gymnasium, you can play. If you are elected Sunday school superintendent year after year, you can play. If you can sing "O Promise Me" in Greek while doing the mazurka, you can play—provided that the congregation loves it, and no one else can do it better.

The Mrs. Wieselvotz Gambit

Assume that you *are* eligible. The case of Mrs. Wieselvotz will give you one example of how the game is played. (Mrs. Wieselvotz is a former Bavarian concert pianist who, by a combination of hard-luck circumstances, has been reduced to playing the organ in a small neighborhood church.)

She begins playing the game of the week on Thursday nights, when she sweeps into choir rehearsal fifteen minutes late. Then she (1) makes a ceremony out of removing her coat, (2) goes over to the director with a look of genuine puzzlement, and (3) says, "Meester Daniels, *vat* iss zat awful noise? Like cats on ze back fence, yowling and yaeling."

"That, Mrs. Wieselvotz, is the choir practicing. As you very well know."

"But vhy don't dey sing then? Dey can stoppen ze varm-up exercises now."

"That *happens* to be what they are singing Sunday."

"Zat? No! Vat iss it called?"

"Ven—When Pants the Hart for Cooling Streams."

"It von't do." Briskly. "I refuse to play such drivia."

"Mrs. Wieselvotz—"

"*No.*"

Silence.

"Vell; fortunately, I have here a luffy little piece you Americans seem to luff."

"We'll try that then. What is it?"

"*Ze Old Oaken Bugget.*"

Complications

Q. What would happen if the choir director were a Prima Donna, too?

A. They might decide to band together against the others, or at least treat each other with professional courtesy—but sooner or later, one of them would end up playing . . .

INSULT

The Basic Philosophy

Let us carry the illustration further, using Mrs. Wieselvotz, although you do not have to be a Prima Donna to play INSULT. Suppose Mrs. Wieselvotz, down in her secret heart, would much rather spend Sunday mornings sitting around with warm feet, listening to *good* music and munching toast, maybe getting out a couple of old scrapbooks instead. But she has an agreement to play the organ, and besides, she can scarcely admit such a wish to herself. What can she do?

She can, by even more irritating and unreasonable behavior, provoke someone else into "insulting" her. (Usually there is no question that she has been insulted, the other party having been genuinely mad enough to play "I Did It and I'm Glad!")

Then she must try to get the rest of the congregation to choose up sides:

"Well, I don't care, he never should have gotten so personal about it; anyone who would call *any*one else a tub of . . ."

"Yes but you didn't see what he had to put up with, week after week after . . ."

The Minister's Part

It is now his turn to play. He can either: (1) Try to soothe things over till next time ("Now, now, Mrs. W., I know he didn't mean what you thought he did"), (2) Get the choir director to apologize or leave the church, or (3) Give Mrs. Wieselvotz the excuse she is looking for to leave.

A variation, when you are more interested in getting someone else out of the church, is "It's Him or Me, Pastor."

The final game in getting your own way is . . .

I'VE GOT A GREAT IDEA!

Breaking and Entering

To play, you need to have some definite ideas on how a church should be run—which isn't as hard as it sounds, since most churches are run rather badly anyway. When you enter a church full of enthusiasm and new ideas, you are usually just

what they need. You may allude mysteriously to your background in Church Administration if you like, but as long as everyone does things your way, this isn't really necessary.

Facing the Opposition

It becomes necessary when somebody opposes you. Not just opposes you, but begins saying things like, "Who does he think he is, anyway!" If it is only one person, you can polish him off with a fast game of INSULT. But if no one wants to make the backyard into a miniature golf course, it is time for you to pack up your ideas and find a place that "really needs you." Not too stable a game, but very ecumenical, particularly if you live in a small town.

Perhaps you are beginning to think that spiritual games are nothing but putting something over on someone else, or fighting. Not at all. The next chapter deals with a favorite indoor sport. In it you will learn "How to Find Out the Latest without Resorting to Idle Gossip."

How to Find Out the Latest
Without Resorting to Idle Gossip

Gossip is a deplorable, silly, indefensible character weakness, reminiscent of Dotty Dripple comic strip types who jabber ceaselessly at the back fence and over the phone. Gossip is something that men almost never stoop to. Gossip never belongs in a Christian church, and it should be properly exorcised. But how in the world are you going to find out what's really going on without gossip?

Although it sounds impossible, there are, actually, two ways:

1. You may become a Railer against Gossip.
2. You may play "Let's All Pray for Poor Mrs. Jensen."

BECOMING A RAILER AGAINST GOSSIP

You must take a vocal stand against gossip, condemning it at every opportunity and protesting how despicable it is to ever discuss other people. If you are a man you can denounce it as a silly female characteristic, but if you are a woman, you must also say things like:

"Great minds talk about ideas, good minds about events, little minds about people," etc.

"Always ask yourself before you speak, 'Is it kind? Is it true? Is it necessary?' Then go ahead—if you still can!"

Exchanging "Confidences"

This may seem exactly opposite to your purposes but it is not, for once everyone is convinced that you are truly against gossiping and would not stoop to it, you are free—not to gossip, but to listen to and exchange high-minded "confidences" about other people; provided, of course, that you always wear a suitably grave and sorrowful expression, as though you are only discussing it for their own good, and regretfully at that.

Look back to the times when you have seen two of the more serious men in your church standing together, shaking their heads and talking in low voices. Did you ever think that what they were saying was gossip? Of course not! And once you have perfected such a technique, rarely if ever will you be called on it.

Akin to RAILER AGAINST GOSSIP, though more basically Christian, is . . .

LET'S ALL PRAY FOR POOR MRS. JENSEN

LAPFPMJ is most often a prayer-meeting game, though it can be played individually if you are considered to be especially spiritual.

Naming the People Involved

In the midweek service, during the time for "prayer requests," somebody must stand up and announce that Mr. Jones has lost his job or that the Browns' son is rebelling and becoming a drunkard, or that two unnamed ladies are fighting again —and would we please remember them in prayer?

This is the time for you to listen carefully; if you are the spokesman, make sure you give all the details, so that everyone can "pray intelligently."

Giving Accurate Details

Do not simply say, "Mr. and Mrs. Deerfield are on the verge of breaking up."

Say, "About three months ago, George began acting suspicious toward the girl who wheeled the coffee wagon into his office. I'm not sure just what type of a girl she was, but evidently . . . " etc. If you are not the spokesman, nudge the person beside you to see if he knows any more about it. Usually someone in the circle will.

Was this what Jesus had in mind when He exhorted us to pray for one another? Nobody knows, though it's always possible.

More techniques of how to gossip without really gossiping will be revealed in the next section, "Helping Others to Be Spiritual."

Helping Others to be Spiritual

Properly speaking, this chapter should not even be necessary. If you are honest and simply tell people what mistakes they are making, what virtues they lack, they will appreciate it and love you for it.

Well, perhaps not *love* you. They may even act as if they dislike you sometimes—but never fear, deep down inside they admire your standards and appreciate your concern for them.

And anyway, aren't Christians warned to expect this kind of treatment from "the crowd"? You're trying to appear spiritual here, not win a popularity contest.

How to Be Above Reproach

To help others, you yourself must naturally be above reproach. That is not to say perfect. No; being above reproach means that you perform everything you do in an adequate,

43

competent, colorless way and possess good personal habits such as brushing your teeth after meals, so that no one will have any reason to criticize *you*.

Allowable Peccadilloes

One or two odd traits are permitted to make you seem human (such as poking around in the offering plate for busfare change if you are a maiden lady, or dozing off during the sermon and snoring if you are an older gentleman). But clearly this game is not for everyone.

Alternately, you may be a loudspoken, intimidating kind of person who castigates everyone, but this somehow shows less finesse than Being Above Reproach and appears less spiritual. And a BAR is usually better at playing . . .

I DON'T MEAN TO CRITICIZE, BUT . . .

The Direct Approach

This form consists of selecting a prefix such as:
"Stop me if I'm wrong, but . . ."
"Perhaps I shouldn't say this, but . . ."
"I don't mean to criticize, but . . ."
and then finishing it with whatever is on your mind. For example:

"Stop me if I'm wrong, George, but haven't you—uh been spending a lot of money on a car?"

"Nope."

"No? You don't think the money could be better used, say, in the leprosy fund?"

"What money? The Lord *gave* me this car in the More-Sudsy Sweepstakes."

The Indirect Approach

There are advantages to using this form. It is more subtle, and safer, since no one can be *really* sure what you're criticizing them about. Make sure though that they have a good idea.

For instance, when you pass one of the elders standing on the church steps smoking on Sunday mornings, cough delicately. Then, when he notices you, chuckle, "Still pounding in the old coffin nails, eh Mr. Jensen?"

Rebuking the Pianist

If you are a person of taste and polish who is jarred in the opening exercises of the Sunday school session by the pianist banging out "The Assurance March" and "I've Got the Joy, Joy, Joy, Joy," go up to her afterward and assure her that she plays exactly like one of your boyhood idols, Big Fats O'Toole and his Ragtime Seven. Make sure, however, that she is a dedicated, spiritual woman who has been playing that way for forty years and will not feel complimented.

Once in a while when you have been trying to help someone else, there will be Repercussions. ("Repercussions" is a particularly Christian word.) To deal with them you should know how to play . . .

I WAS ONLY TRYING TO HELP

IOWTH comes afterward, when someone else has heard angry reports of your efforts or has had her shoulder cried on. You may find your first reaction is indignation at having your well-meant efforts taken the wrong way, but you must quell

45

this unspiritual reaction in a sweet-marshmallowy response. So that when Mrs. Makewell asks you, "Did you say anything to Myrna Smith about the casserole she brought?"

"Casserole?"

"That it tasted like dogfood?"

"No. I didn't."

"Oh."

" 'Horsemeat,' I said."

"Well, maybe you shouldn't have said anything. She says she isn't coming back."

"Well, why not? I was only trying to *help*."

Perhaps you feel that this type of individualistic effort is not quite your style. Perhaps, you say, you are a nicer, more discreet type of person, who would not dream of saying anything unkind. That's fine, if you want to be like that. But if you *do* like the idea of "guardian" games and are just a little bit timid, you haven't been forgotten. You can still help, within the safety of a group, by "Holding the Fort against Heresy."

Holding the Fort Against Heresy

Ever since the Albigenses were burned at the stake, the Christian Church has been engaged in a battle against creeping liberalism. (Liberalism is not always theological; it may come in the form of a group that wants to discard Evening Prayer and set up a Religious Panel Discussion instead.) Take a good look around you: Are certain words creeping into the conversation, words like ecumenical and situation ethics? Is your minister starting to memorize jokes from *Playboy* magazine? Is there a paperback hidden behind the pew, a wisp of smoke from under the Ladies Room door? If so, you've got trouble.

What Can Be Done About It

Short of making sure that everything around you, the people you know, the books and magazines you read, are completely pure (a nearly impossible undertaking because of the weakness of human nature), either you must become resigned to the prevailing evil, or you should play . . .

47

HOLDING THE FORT

Locating Other Heresy Hunters

The best thing about playing HTF is that there is always a like-minded group of players for you to join. Indeed, you cannot very well play alone without being thought of as having a persecution complex. So if you are a woman you must locate this gathering, usually in the foyer or in a prominent corner of the missionary society tea. HTF-ers are almost always wearing respectably long, rather lumpy suits or dresses, Decent Hats and Sensible Shoes. They come in all shapes and sizes, but commonly on the shady side of fifty. Younger potential players are too busy still trying to whip their husbands and children into line. (Regular players have husbands too, but they have usually won or given up by now.)

Recognizing Their Conversation

Most of all, you can tell them by their talk. They secretly believe that the golden days of real Christianity are over, and huddle together as the last true remnant of believers, guardians of the faith. For instance:

"So I said to her, listen, I said, you know as well as I do that no divorced man is *ever* really the inno—"

". . . her skirt nearly up to her *waist,* and looking as brazen as you please!"

"Of course, I have to *laugh,* it was so . . ."

"I told him pointblank, if you consider the great hymns of the church outdated, then you can just . . ."

Group Benefits

The advantages of huddling together in such a group are obvious. Not only are you able to strengthen one another's feelings and confirm one another's worst fears, you are able, as a cabal, to tackle any proposed "changes" in the church. And, by one concerted glance, you can properly wither anyone who is trespassing on the grass.

The Male Version

If you are a man wishing to play HTF you will have more important concerns. You will have to decide: Which seminaries are going liberal? What can be done to clean up the shelves of the local library? Why has the minister been counseling that young divorcee so much lately?

And, of course, you will be busy . . .

OPPOSING NEWFANGLED "GIMMICKS"

You have been teaching the junior boys Sunday school class for the last thirty years, mumbling the lesson from the manual and giving pencils for Christmas, when suddenly the superintendent comes up and informs you about the new teacher-training course. Even though he smiles at you nervously, trying to be nice, you can tell what he is up to—and you must have it out.

Having It Out

Look him in the eye and say, "What's the matter with the way I teach? It may not be that great—but I'm doing the best I can."

"No, no! We just thought you might be . . ."

"Nothing like experience, I always say."

By standing firm against any modern "gimmicks" you are able to get out of a lot of unnecessary work and study.

A variation of this game is "But This Is the Way We've *Always* Done It."

Now that you have learned how to handle the congregation, you must learn "What to Do When You Know More than the Minister."

What to Do When You Know
More than the Minister

This is not really a problem, since most people are sure they know more than the minister anyway. (Not in theology, of course, but in the sordid knowledge of *real* life. Since ministers are never tempted to swear, enjoy sex, or cheat on their income tax return, they do not even realize that such things go on all the time, and therefore you are one up on them.) Actually, it is a rather pleasant position to be in, since it exempts you from all sorts of obligations. You don't even have to know any theology to play . . .

I DIDN'T GET A THING OUT OF IT

Your Cue to Begin Playing IDGATOOI IS:

1. When the minister stops telling heart-warming stories about self-sacrificing children, about animals who died heroi-

cally while saving their master, or no longer recites the poem about the battered violin ("The Touch of the Master's Hand") and begins preaching.

2. When the guest speaker stops telling jokes and "gets down to business."

3. When the missionary from Africa, with all the wonderful "illustrations" he could have given of cannibals and narrow escapes with snakes, gets up and preaches a *sermon* instead!

4. When the minister says something you don't want to hear, or mentions a shock-word such as tithing or integrating-*this*-church.

5. When the minister doesn't have a Ph.D. and you do.

6. When the minister goes over his allotted fifteen minutes.

Possible Exceptions

Anyone from England, who speaks with a decidedly British accent, is automatically exempt. You must turn out whenever one is in the vicinity for a special service and in all cases say afterward, "*Such* a blessing. I got so much out of it, I could have listened to him talk for hours!" Whether you understood him or not is immaterial here.

Continuing the Game

This game is concluded on the steps of the church, or sitting around the Sunday dinner table.

"Who wants more potatoes? Bill?"

"*You* do. Ha-ha."

"Here."

"Help yourself first."

54

"Oh no. If I eat another bite, I'll burst."

"Well, save them till after church, ha, ha, ha."

"Oh. You know, I hate to say this, but I didn't get a *thing* out of that missionary this morning. I was planning to go tonight, of course, but in a way it seems silly to waste the time. I mean, if I'm not going to get anything out of it anyway. Why don't you and the kids go?"

"Are you sure? What are you going to do?"

"Oh, just rest." (Do not say that *The F.B.I.* looks interesting.)

Other Benefits

Also, by playing this game, you can feel automatically absolved of any responsibility you might have felt toward anything *in* the message; the best players are often self-styled Bible scholars, who have attended a year or so of Bible school, and know more than the minister anyway.

After you have had practice in IDGATOOI and feel especially ambitious, you may want to continue with . . .

ISN'T IT TRUE THAT . . .

Educational Background

If your education has not primed you with more facts about more subjects than nearly everyone else, you should pick out a few topics, such as the implications of the Mauer Jaw and Peking Tooth for modern apologetics or The Art of Curling Beards (the person, *not* the profession), and bone up on them.

Then you are ready to pounce on the minister/missionary/

guest speaker, letting him know how much *you* know and forcing him to feel inadequate or to recognize you as a happy combination of Calvin, Aquinas, and St. Paul.

A few cases may best illustrate IITT.

The J. Alfred Prufrock Gambit

Sidle up to your minister and say cryptically, "I grow old. I grow old. I shall wear the bottoms of my trousers rolled."

If he does not respond immediately with "Shall I part my hair in front? Do I dare to eat a peach?" you can write him off as "shockingly illiterate." One test quote a week should do the trick.

Approaching the Missionary

During the Missionary Conference, stroll over to the table of exhibits, pick up a shrunken head, and say casually to the missionary who owns it, "Isn't it generally true that anomie along the Amazon has risen sharply with the heat and, conversely, with the waning of the *pupuelus?*"

Pause while he attempts to figure out what you are talking about, then nod your head gently, say "I *thought* so," and move on.

The Obscure Theologian Gambit

Every Sunday, of course, gives you another opportunity to pass the minister at the door. While shaking his hand, declare, "Isn't it true that the point you made about baptismal edification was also cited in the late seventh century by Herr Vanderpeel, the Belgian theologian?"

"Why-uh, yes, I believe it was."

"I *thought* so! Now, can you refresh my memory as to which volume it was in?"

This is, of course, tricky, since he might just answer "Why, the third" without batting an eyelash. But usually he will admit he doesn't know.

On the other hand, every once in a while you may come across a minister who counters with the game . . .

YES, AND DID YOU KNOW?

To your initial question he may also respond, "Yes, and did you know that old Vanderpeel had quite a bit to say about baptismal *rejuvenation?*"

The missionary may inform you that the *main* cause of all the trouble is a small, bedbuglike creature called the Amazonian mudrack.

And if, when you sidle up to the minister with "In the room the women come and go" and he responds with "The purple cow rides high tonight," you can never really be sure that he is making it up, that he has not actually located some early obscure volume of Eliot poems.

But now that you have learned to manage most situations that arise in church, you will want to know how to achieve "Instant Status."

Instant Status Games

Achieving status is not exactly a Christian grace, such as practicing forbearance or loving your neighbor. As a matter of fact, it is not a Christian grace at all. It is a secular idea, dreamed up by some sociologist, and one that Christians do not worry about. The only time Christians worry about status is when they find they don't have enough.

When You Lack Status

Perhaps, even though you have been playing many of the games, you feel that not everybody is convinced. Or maybe you have simply been playing too much SALESMAN and not enough HOLDING THE FORT. In any case, the first game which should correct the situation and enhance your status is . . .

TROPHY

Q. Who is eligible to play TROPHY?

A. Any former convict, opera singer, socialite, movie star, headhunter, football hero, or participant in the St. Valentine's Day Massacre, who has been dramatically converted.

The Basic Philosophy

In many religious circles your status is already secure, based on the reasoning that: (1) If someone like *you* was saved, there's got to be something there, and (2) If it's good enough for a celebrity like you, all nonsocialite, nonopera singer non-Christians will see that it's certainly good enough for them, and be converted too.

But, most important, you are a clearly recognizable "Trophy of Grace"—which means that you will be able to spend the rest of your life singing, touring, and "giving your testimony" at church gatherings, Christian banquets, and youth rallies. You will be interviewed by Sunday school papers and, perhaps, have a movie made of your life. The one thing to remember is to paint a detailed picture of your former life and degradation. If you were a gang fighter, point out all the scars on your arm and describe with some gusto the fights in which you received them. If you were an aspiring singer or movie star, emphasize how much you have given up (fame and adulation, the Academy Awards, a heart-shaped swimming pool), for your Faith.

Retaining Your Trappings

Unlike some other games, equipment is rather important. The handcuffs you wore to jail, the spear you used to kill other tribes with—these are what make your story so effective. Don't throw away your theatrical makeup or your pink tuxedo, if you were a performer. Christians are delighted to "make allowances" in such cases, enjoying a certain superiority and vicarious thrill, and saying, "Poor fellow, he doesn't *know* any different." So you are quite free to be yourself, if that is yourself. Remember, looking the part is much of the game.

If there is no way for you to play TROPHY, you may want to try . . .

AS I WAS SAYING TO BILLY (GRAHAM) THE OTHER DAY

AIWSTB(G)TOD is a relatively mild game, ego-rewarding and rather pleasant, since other people can play it back, creating a general state of importance all around. On the other hand, it *can* be used to keep other people in their place.

Selecting Your Symbol

When all the "in" people went to Wheaton College/speak in tongues/take a Holy Land tour to Palestine every spring, they can make the rest of the congregation feel a little beneath them because *they* haven't been to Mecca too.

Or, if you are a respectable, status-seeking minister, you can substitute "As I was saying to Bishop Kennedy/Karl Barth/Paul Tournier . . ." depending on what circle you happen to move in. Or Princeton or Union vs. Moody Bible Institute. Or even *Christianity and Crisis* vs. *Together.**

The possibilities and the rewards are infinite. The next game, also rewarding but a little more work, is . . .

MY BIBLE'S MORE UNDERLINED THAN YOURS

Do Not Be Deceived by the Name

Even if you've never opened a Bible in your life, you can play. The object is to do anything other Christians do, only more so and better. That is, bake more cakes, memorize more Scripture verses, entertain more bishops, roll more bandages, buy more theological textbooks, know more piano hymn-runs, supervise more boys club baseball games or clothing drives than anyone else you know.

And, if you want to go one step further, you can play . . .

MARY MARTYR

The Basic Philosophy

Although this is not confined to women, they are usually a little better at it. In every church there is at least one player who will take all kinds of thankless jobs upon herself, even if she is really much too busy, seemingly without a word of complaint—except for her pale and drawn face, the darkening circles under her eyes.

"Mary Martyr" is the one who stays after the missionary tea and does all the dishes, types all the office work when there

* See "How to Play Christian Magazine Subscriber."

is no secretary, and volunteers to drive all the Pioneer Girls home. And status is often the least of her surface considerations though it is of course there.

Q. Who else plays this game?

A. The congregation, who must keep saying, "Isn't Mary wonderful; I can't imagine *what* we'd do without her!" Then they must unselfishly continue to load work upon her until:

1. She collapses and they say, "I had no *idea* she had a nervous condition."

2. She realizes she is being used, causing her to become extremely bitter and refuse to do anything.

3. Some kind soul who isn't playing tries to relieve her of her overload—which ruins everything.

Answering Youth
and Other Doubters

Sooner or later, in trying to appear spiritual, you will come across some vexing moral problems. You may discover them yourself or others may call them to your attention—sometimes even coming to you for guidance. The thing to do is not to panic; in order to allay suspicion, all you need to do is memorize these Perfect Christian Responses.

You should understand, of course, that the Perfect Christian Responses are time-honored and classic, that they have been passed down through generations as answers to life's problems, and though they might seem a little shopworn or inadequate, they are actually very helpful and have been keeping Christian youth in their place for years.

You will notice, in the following illustrative situations, that all are concerned with answering the problems raised by youth. Such intellectual doubters, especially those who are long-haired, arrogant, and forever blowing pipesmoke in your face, can be most trying—unless you happen to be one. If you are, then you already know what to say.

Answering Evolution

Situation: You are peacefully dozing in the Sunday school class you teach, listening to the mumble of the lesson, when in comes The Rebel back from college. Sunday morning, and here he is in a sweater and *jeans.* "Mr. Jensen, if man has certain characteristics resembling Plesiadapidae and if the taxonomic approximation of the Hominidae and the Pongidae in a common superfamily represents a natural classification, wouldn't the assumption follow that the two families are ultimately derived through the process of divergent modification?"

Answer: "*You* can think you descended from an ape if you want, but *I* didn't."

Guiding Your Impressionable Daughter

Situation: Your teenage daughter is going out with somebody new. You don't know what her plans are, but you want to find out tactfully. You say, "Just where do you think *you're* going tonight?"

"Out. To a movie."

"*What* movie?"

"*Mondo Cane.* It's an art film."

"I don't like the sound of *that.*"

"Do you speak Italian? You don't even know what it's about."

"Okay, just answer me one question and I'll be satisfied."

"What's that?"

"Can you take Jesus with you to see it?"

The Up-and-Outers Gambit

Situation: You are standing in the back of the church, a few minutes before the service, when The Rebel comes over to you. "Say, Mr. Tucker," he says, "if you're a Christian, how come you live in a sixty-thousand-dollar house, have two cars, a color television set, and a cleaning woman when other people right in this town are out of work and starving to death? And some, because of lack of money, have never even heard of Christianity? Didn't Christ preach *against* materialism? Didn't He tell the rich young ruler to go sell all he had and give it to the poor? How can you justify that?"

Answer: There is no reason to get angry. Remain calm and say simply, "Let me ask you a question. Suppose everyone did sell their belongings like you say; do you honestly think that people of means would be attracted to such a shoddy, lower-class type of Christianity?"

"I don't—"

"Of course not. Some of us are called to be a testimony to the *up*-and-outers."

Helping the Weaker Brother

Situation: You are the president of the Christian fellowship group at your college. A knock sounds on your door and in walks a troubled sophomore, another member. "I just don't *know* any more," he confesses. "The more I study, the more I find the whole idea of Christianity, the *Logos* idea, incredible, except as a twisted myth. Heaven; eternal life; it's all too perfect, it's incredible! You know what I had to do last Sunday? I had to walk out of the Communion service because I found I

70

didn't believe it anymore. What am I going to do? Where do I go from here?"

Answer: Ease up from your desk, walk casually over to the sophomore. Hands on hips, stand for a second scrutinizing him. Then, decisively, you act. Give him a warm, friendly grin, a very hardy slap on the back. "Cheer up, old Buddy," you announce in get-well tones, "everybody has doubts!"

SPECIAL CHRISTIAN SKILLS

How to Play Good
Christian Letterwriter

To Let Them Know You're a Good Christian,
Write Good Christian Letters

Have you ever known a Good Christian who could not write a Good Christian letter? Of course not. If one wants to be a Good Christian, one must not only know how to read in order to memorize Scripture verses; one must know how to write in order to express his spirituality through Christian letters. Christian letters are as indispensable as knowing what to say.*

Here is how to go about writing your very own Christian letter.

---

* See "Perfect Response Games."

Assemble Materials

Ballpoint pen; stationery; envelopes; verse stickers and/or slogan stickers; Bible and/or a handy leaflet listing the Most Used Verses (in order to expedite things). The stationery cannot be plain stationery with pictures of flowers or dogs or other pretty things unless your letter must go out in the next mail and you are caught without *Christian stationery*. Christian stationery is stationery with pictures of flowers or dogs or other pretty things *plus* embossed Bible verses usually in gold that has partly flaked off.

For instance, on cute notepaper-type stationery, instead of a plain puppy dog wagging his tail at the top left-hand side of the paper, there will be a puppy dog wagging his tail and barking in little gold flaking letters, *"Rejoice in the Lord alway, and again I say Rejoice!"* However, if you are caught without Christian stationery, it is possible to take plain stationery and to write beside the plain puppy dog, as fancily as you can in your own handwriting, *"Rejoice, Etc!"*

Select the Salutation

After your materials are assembled, but before you write one word, you must decide what kind of Good Christian you are going to be. In some cases this determines the salutations and texts you will need to use; in other cases it won't make any difference anyway. Nonetheless, check. Do you want to play Good Upper Middle Class Sophisticated but Friendly Christian Letterwriter? If so, you must now discard the cute puppy dog paper and begin all over again with top-grade, medium-sized, white or beige letter sheets with *no* dogs, and the "Re-

joice" engraved in non-flaking gold script that shows Good Taste.

But to get on with the game: What kind of Christian? Theological? Heartsy? The whole point is that if you are playing it heartsy and woman, you want to open as a heartsy woman; for instance:

"My dear little chicken in the Lord"

Or: "My dear and precious sister in . . ."

On the other hand, if you want to play middle-aged male codger who is given to firm theological stands, those greetings may sound a little silly.

Of late "Dear Friend in Christ" is usually reserved for those wishing to play Seller-of-Christian-Wares-Through-a-Mailing.

Refine the Contents

Generally, Christian letters tend to be heavy. In fact, wordy. No matter what the subject is, certain phrases and terms must be worked into the context, or it won't be a Good Christian letter.

Rules to Follow

Do Not Say:
"I hope you are over the flu."
Do Say:
"I earnestly pray that God is stretching His mighty hand toward you in your illness and that you will soon be happy and healthy in Him. (The precept may sometimes be that a prayer spoken of is a prayer prayed, and thus you are performing two duties at the same time.)
Do Not Say:
"The mission board rejected me as a candidate because I flunked the preliminary qualification tests."

Do Say:

"Despite much labor, love, prayer, and plans, the Lord has, in His infinite wisdom, seen fit to *close the door* to the mission field . . ."

Do Not Say:

"I'm expecting a baby in April."

Do Say:

"We are praying that God will send a precious little new soul into our family by the time the robins sing again."

Do Not Say:

"Please return your overdue books to the church library."

Do Say:

"As our church librarian, I do earnestly trust that you will remember to return the fine choice of Christian books you borrowed from our shelves so that others may feed upon . . ."

Do Not Say:

"We bought a new candy-apple red Mustang last Thursday. Wowie!"

Do Say:

"A week and three days ago, God in His mercy provided us with a small automobile which we hope and trust will be used greatly in the service of picking up and discharging the neighborhood children to and from Sunday school."

Do Not Say:

"Since I wrote you last Christmas, Clyde's mother has come to live with us. What a life!"

Do Say:

"Since last Christmas we have been given a new cross to bear. Clyde's dear aged mother has come to live out her remaining days on earth with . . ."

Prepare the Enclosures

To fit out the Christian letter, in some circles it is considered a necessity to include a leaflet, a bookmark with a quotation from the Bible or Augustine, or at least a page torn out of a daily devotional guide. Stacks of tracts are printed each year and of course it is sinful to let these go to waste. If you have accumulated a supply by all means use them before the bookmarks etc. Most leaflets are intended for nonbelievers, but somehow it seems safer to send them to people already in the fold. The reasons are obvious. Those in the fold will be impressed with your thoughtfulness and spirituality, while the chance exists that those outside will think you are a little batty. Don't take that chance: *send Christian tracts to Christians.*

Follow the example of one pastor who keeps a pile of tracts Christians have sent to him on his desk, all ready to send to other Christians. In the last six months, each of his elders has received, gently tucked in with the pastoral communique, "You Don't *Dare* Believe!"; "I Was a Beatle Fan"; "How to Save Your Marriage"; "Is Life Worth It?" and "Hell Is Waiting."

Add the Complimentary Closing

In creating the closing of a Christian letter, use imagination. Surely you can think of something even better than:

"Farewell and all fond regards until in the circle of faith we meet again to perform the good works allotted to us"
Or:
"The late hour bids me close but my prayers and hope and love and thoughts will be constantly with you"
Or:
"Yours in the loving faithful joy of His wonderful, dedicated service . . ."

How to Be a Christian
Magazine Subscriber

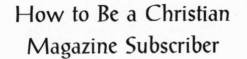

Why Subscribe?

Have you ever known a Good Christian who did not subscribe to several religious periodicals? Of course not. Anyone
who has been moved to tears by the poem "If Jesus Came to
Your House" knows that an important part of being spiritual
consists of exhibiting spiritual literature. This is why some
Christians know of the panic to hide *Esquire* and substitute
Christian Life, to sit on *Time* and hold *Eternity* in the lap, to
bury *Consumer's Report* under *Guideposts* on the coffee table
when another Christian unexpectedly drops by.

How to Subscribe to the Right Magazine

Survey *first,* subscribe *after* is the rule here. It is absolutely
necessary to check around your church and with people who

belong to the organizations you attend to find out which publications are acceptable. Nothing is more disturbing than to become an avid reader of *Moody Monthly* only to discover that the most popular people get *Christian Century*. Or, on the other hand, that the important people fill their magazine racks with *Christian Life* while you made the mistake of ordering *Christianity Today*. Subscribing to the same magazine as everyone else around you is the unavoidable criterion.

What to Do with It When You've Got It

To read it or not to read it—that's the decision you make when the magazine comes through the mail. Many are convinced that a Christian magazine serves its full purpose when it is owned and displayed in the same way as a mink coat or a set of the *Encyclopaedia Britannica*. Actually *reading* the magazine seems of minor importance. Still, if you feel you want to, you can always play one of the two general reader's games, DEVOTEE or GREAT CRITIC.

DEVOTEE

A "Devotee" is a reader who reads everything in a periodical as if the entire magazine were inspired and infallible. This is often played by someone who believes that all the news fit to print is published only by his own denomination.

To play DEVOTEE you should read one article each day of the month in the periodical(s) chosen. You may consider yourself successful if you cover the daily article and nod in virtuous assent at the conclusion of it. For extra spiritual credit, before you attend the men's or women's society, take note of a sentence you have read that will enrich others. Any sentence will do, such as (Example 1*) a reviewer's quotation of John Robinson's latest work to (Example 2*) a fact you have gleaned from the advertisements.

Imagine the impression you will make when, at the church meeting, you turn to your neighbor and say: "Is not the church an archaic and well-protected institution for the preservation of something that is irrelevant and incredible?" Or: "Did you realize our women's society could make from $170 to $2000 if we let Blotto Candy help us!"

GREAT CRITIC

This game is harder to play than DEVOTEE. First, to complicate things, you have to know that there are two varieties of Great Critics—those who ferret out heresy and new ideas, and those who miss the point completely. Often a heresy hunter becomes so adept that he can judge a magazine just by smelling it. A well-trained nose is able to discern faulty logic, sacrilegious flippancy, and haughty originality on contact.

If you are playing heresy-and-new-ideas hunter, you will waste no time when you have smelled such an article. You will write the editor. The best of Christian foibles may be at stake.

* *Example 1*, the reviewer's quotation: "The Bishop in his book asks, 'Is not the church an archaic and well-protected institution for the preservation of something that is irrelevant and incredible?' "

* *Example 2*, the fact from the advertisement: "Your Women's Society can make from $170 to $2000 If You Let Blotto Candy Help You!"

If you would like to play "Point Misser," you must first scan the magazine of your choice for words such as *cosmetics, intellectual, wine, brotherhood, Roman Catholic, Negro, Jew,* etc. Without reading the author's meaning (actually without reading the article at all) you can immediately assume that the author is *against* cosmetics, intellectuals, wine, brotherhood, Roman Catholics, Negroes, Jews, etc. If he *weren't* against them, why would he bother to mention them at all?

Hurry; write a letter to the editor and give him the very devil for being narrow, shortsighted, and prejudiced.

For all who want to play GREAT CRITIC of any variety, here is a convenient list of phrases to help you draft your letter:

1. "Dear Editor—if you still have the nerve to call yourself one . . ."

2. "What warped minds you must have! Can you honestly believe that any genuine Christian cares more for a new home than he does for the Lord? I have been a Christian for thirty years and have never met such a man as your article describes. Besides, if I happen to have the money to buy a new home, it is only because the Lord *blessed* me with the money to buy . . ."

3. "How dismayed we were to discover that our favorite magazine had published an article on unwed mothers. Are not our children exposed to enough immorality already from the *world?* Are they to discover the *Church* is concerned with it too? . . ."

4. "When I saw that the fiction story you chose for April carried the word 'make-up' three times and the word 'cosmetics' twice, I threw your magazine in the wastecan without even reading it. You would think that even the most *backward* Christian would be beyond judging spirituality by outward appearances as your author did in his story . . ."

5. "I have been giving your magazine to an unsaved friend for whom I am praying, trusting it will be used to help her to a decision. Sadly, before I could give her the latest issue, I had to tear

85

off the cover which showed a young girl painted up with lipstick and rouge . . ."

6. "What do you mean 50% of all Christians need a psychiatrist? *You're* the one who needs a psychiatrist . . ."

7. "The Lord has led me to cancel my . . ."

PARAPHERNALIA

Serve the Lord with gladness . . . (Psalm 100:2)

Main Street Church

1 Main Street   Phone: 453-0950

GLAD TIDINGS

A Friendly Memo Published Weekly

⸺•⟐•⸺

Pastor: John J. Mainer, Th.M.

VERSE OF THE WEEK:

Serve the Lord with gladness . . . (Psalm 100:2)

**How *You* Can Serve the Lord
with Gladness—May 4 thru May 10**

Coming Events of the Week

MONDAY, May 4

10:00 A.M.   *Ladies Circle*. All of our ladies are invited to meet with Mrs. Blanche Minniver to cut out and paste bird pictures on Bible verse cards. These bird cards are for distribution on hospital trays and bring joy to the patients. Bring any old magazines with pictures of birds you have around the house. Here is your chance for a *unique creative challenge!!*

6:00 P.M.   *Missionary Supper*. DON'T MISS IT! The Mary-Martha class will serve a covered-dish supper in honor of our hometown-born missionary NINA BLACK-FERN. On furlough from Darkest Africa, Nina possesses an extensive collection of Elephantiasis and Goiter slides, and she has promised to show them all for us. Let's show her our love by a *large turnout!*

7:30 P.M.   *Deacons' Meeting* at Deacon Sloop's house. Deaconesses will furnish light refreshments please.

TUESDAY, May 5

7:00 P.M.   *Important Meeting for Building Committee* in the Pastor's study. Building Committee wives will furnish punch and cookies please.

8:30 P.M.   *Trustees Meeting.* "Coffee 'n' Cake" to be provided by Trustee wives, please.

WEDNESDAY, May 6

8:00 P.M.   Do you CARE about PRAYER??? If so you won't miss our *weekly prayer and Bible study time.* Pastor Mainer has planned a long and interesting talk on Old Testament Genealogy.

THURSDAY, May 7

TODAY IS THE DAY! ! ! ! !

The floors are laid in the church basement; the electrician has put in the lights, and the new cooking stoves were left (by mistake) on Deacon Sloop's front porch yesterday. BUT! Much remains to be done. *Men!* We need you! Come early and stay late!

NOTE: Regular meeting of the *Men's Service Guild* will not be held since the men will be working in the basement. HOWEVER: Officers will meet at 6:30 for a short executive session on Deacon Sloop's front porch. (If you own a truck big enough to load a stove on, please bring it to this meeting.)

HOT FOOD! Served for the basement workers at 11:00 P.M. by the women of the *Glad Tidings Bible Class*. (Ladies, please make sure all the tables are back in place and the dishes done after the men are finished eating, thank you!)

FRIDAY, May 8

8:00 A.M.   *Glad Tidings Bible Class* meets with Mrs. Mainer. BE AWAKE and COME PREPARED. Ladies, you can't afford to let other things crowd out your study of the Word of God!

12:00 NOON   *Businessmen's Luncheon*. Wives of the Businessmen have promised an excellent repast!

7:00 P.M.   *Choir Rehearsal*. Director Munse sends an urgent call for sweet-voiced sopranos and strong basses. If you have a talent, don't sit back; *use* it for the Lord.

8:00 P.M.   *Youth Conference* up at Hallowed Lake. We *still* need three CHAPERONES and four DRIVERS. Here is your opportunity for JOYFUL SERVICE.

The YPers plan to arrive at the lake by 9:00 P.M., pitch camp in the dark, sleep under the stars until 5:00 or 6:00 A.M. when they will be up and running for a full day of lively activity.

To be young again yourself, be up at the lake with them.

8:00 P.M.   *Finance Committee* begins its House-to-House COMMITMENT CAMPAIGN. We still need $3,000 to finish the basement. If the Lord lays on *your* heart any name for the COMMITMENT LIST we don't have, please contact the finance chairman immediately. Thank you.

(Refreshments by the Finance Committee wives after the trek!)

SATURDAY, May 9

A MOST IMPORTANT DAY

An all-day meeting of the *Community Sunday School Commission*. Let's show our spirit of cooperation by outstanding representation from our church! LADIES OF MAIN STREET CHURCH: It's your turn to put on the CSSC Luncheon this time. If you haven't been solicited, call Mrs. H. Bloodstone to see how you can help!

SUNDAY, May 10

Six days for pleasure and self.
DOESN'T GOD DESERVE AT LEAST *ONE* DAY OUT OF YOUR BUSY WEEK??
Following are a list of services at our church . . .

How to Play Altar Guild President...

... in the midst of a great crisis as shown from the President's own notes pilfered from her handbag after the regular meeting of St. Mary's Guild on April 10, 19xx.

```
Mary Potts, President. My Notes. Meeting Here, Apr. 10.
(Remember: Call Sarah and borrow more silver teaspoons so
Mrs. Claybody isn't insulted by having to use a stainless
one.)
  1. Call the meeting to order.
  2. Open with prayer.
     Our ~~God~~ Father, we ~~want to ask~~ beseech ~~You~~ Thee to be
     present and ~~get us through~~ assist us in all ~~our~~
     ~~troubles our arguments~~ our activities, and by ~~some~~
     ~~weird miracle~~ Thy great mercies, endow our members
     with the ~~ambition the~~ will to ~~get the Altar brass all~~
     ~~polished before Easter. to~~ complete the task Thou
     hast given us to do in Thy Chancel.
                         ~~For Christ's Sake~~
                         ~~In the Name of Our Lord and~~
                         Through Jesus Christ our Lord.
                         Amen
```

97

3. Sec'ys Report. (Say: Will someone move to approve as read, thank you very much.)

4. Treasurer's Report. (Say the same thing, thank you very much.)

5. Old Business.

Old Business A: Polishing the Brass for Easter.

1. Say very calmly: It's only one week before Easter, and only Esther Tome and Jinny Nobbins showed up in the Sacristy yesterday to work on the Brass, and there are 22 separate candlesticks, crosses, etc. to polish yet, and two silver Communion services to clean. Tactfully try to get it across to Claybody that she can't Pour at the Easter Monday Tea unless she gets busy with the Maundy Thursday Polishing Cloth.

Old Business B: About Calling Father Boon Father.

1. If Mrs. Boon is there, don't bring it up.

2. If she isn't there, mention carefully. Say: As we discussed at the last meeting, our new Rector would prefer to be called "Father" and he wishes the Altar Guild would set an example for the congregation; then Smile gently.

3. If Nelly Jones says we're going down the Road to Rome, ask Betty Bufferfield to explain that at least six churches in this Deanery call their rectors "Father" and they are all perfectly good churches with nice, low services.

4. If Mrs. Rudge says she's been in this parish for 50 years and every rector here has always been happy to be called "Mr.," don't answer back.

5. If no one says anything for a period of 30 seconds, Smile around the room and say: So we are all agreed to set an example for the congregation, etc. Thank you.

6. New Business.

New Business A: The Junior Altar Guild

1. If Esther Tome is there, don't bring it up.

2. If she isn't there, say tactfully: Some members of the Junior Altar Guild whose mother we all know well were caught parading around the church in the Rector's best Alb

when they were supposed to be on Altar Duty, and what
should we do about it??????

3. If Mrs. Boon tries to smooth it over by saying kids
will be kids, mention tactfully how <u>hard it is to wash and
iron</u> the Rector's best Alb.

4. If Betty B. lets on that she thinks Esther T. will
quit the Guild if we do anything drastic to stop her kids
from raising the devil, <u>drop the subject</u> until after Easter
when the Brass is all polished.

5. Ask for motion that discussion be waived from the
Secy's minutes, Thank you.

<u>New Business B:</u> Altar Duty for May.

1. If Jinny Nobbins is there, don't bring it up.

2. If she isn't there, mention tactfully that the lady
who signed up for May Altar Duty always sets up the Communion with two cruets full of wine and no cruet of water,
and no Chalice, and what are we going to do about it because she means so well??????

3. If no one suggests anything, wink at Betty B. and
have her make a motion that Mrs. Boon go on Duty in May with
the lady who already signed up, and teach her how to set
up the Communion.

4. If Nelly J. lets on she thinks Jinny N. will quit the
Guild if we put Mrs. Boon up to telling her she's forgotten
the water and the Chalice all this time, <u>drop the subject</u>
until after Easter when the Brass is all polished.

5. Ask for motion to waive disc. from Secy's minutes,
Thank you.

<u>Say Is there</u> any other New Business?

1. If it's 3:30 already, don't give them a chance to
bring up any more new business; say:

Will someone please move the meeting be adjourned?

2. If Mrs. Boon is there, ask her to close with prayer.

3. If she isn't there, say,

Our Father who art in Heaven
Hallowed be Thy Name and so forth.

4. Then say: Refreshments are ready in the dining room.

Mrs. Claybody, I'd be delighted if you would take charge of the Tea Table for us. By the way that reminds me of our Easter Monday Tea at the Parish House. Are you planning on being there? We hope to decide who will preside at _that_ Tea Table when we _all_ get together to polish the Brass on Maundy Thursday. You surely won't miss being with us, will you??????

What Kind of a Christian Are You?

Here is a short quiz that will tell you what kind of a Christian you are, fanatic, liberal, etc. Check the answer that comes closest to matching your own feelings. At the end of the exam is a key to tell you how to score yourself.

Multiple Choice (Choose one answer only):

1.   You are visiting a new acquaintance who, in the course of conversation, offers you a glass of beer. You say:

A——"Oh, no thank you, I *don't drink*. But you go ahead—if you want." Be nice about it, but make sure they get a copy of *A Drunkard's Grave, or That Demon Rum!*

B——"Oh, yes please!" then think giddily to yourself, "Look at me! I'm a Christian. I'm drinking beer. Isn't this beer delicious!"

C——"If you don't mind, I'd rather have Jack Daniels."

2.   If asked to define a Christian movie, you would say:

A——Where Redd Harper sings, and everybody gets saved.

B——Any film within the Judeo-Christian context. *Cat on a Hot Tin Roof* is *basically Christian.*

C——*The Greatest Story Ever Told*, with John Wayne playing the Centurion at the cross.

3.   You have just found out that your best friend is "speaking in tongues." Your reaction is:

A——People who speak in tongues are crazy.

B——People who speak in tongues *may* have a deeper religious experience. The ones who are Episcopalians, *not* Pentecostals.

C——There may be nothing wrong with it, but would you want your daughter to marry one?

4.   The man up the street from you, a real estate salesman, has suddenly been doing so well that he has had a swimming pool installed and just bought a Rolls Royce. As a Christian, your response is:

A——"The rain may fall on the just and unjust, but someday he'll get his."

B——"Something's rotten in Denmark."

C——Congratulate him when you see him, then try to find out what church he belongs to—with an eye to joining.

5.   If asked to define a Catholic, you would say:

A——Catholics are those people who have little statues on their dashboards and play Bingo in church.

B——A few Catholics may sneak into heaven, but most of them are planning on going to purgatory.

C——A Catholic is a Christian who believes too many things.

6.   If asked to define a Jew, you would say:
A——The Jews used to be God's chosen people.
B——Jews are people about whom you say some of my best friends are.
C——The Jews are all going back to Palestine, so don't worry about them anyway.

7.   If asked to define a Buddhist, you would say:
A——One of those people who wear sandals and speak Zen.
B——A practitioner of an ancient and honorable philosophic system. Buddhists are inscrutable but wrong.
C——Someone who lives in Buddha.

8.   When asked to define a miracle, you would say:
A——A supernatural event in the Bible, such as the feeding of the five thousand. The age of miracles is over.
B——What many people consider to be a supernatural event, but in actuality may be attributed to an underlying natural cause.
C——Getting a seat in a half-jammed theater.

[Scoring key on page 106]

HOW TO SCORE:

Count up the number of A, B, and C answers that you checked.

If most of your answers are A, you are a Christian, all right, but bordering on the fanatic. It is one thing to act spiritual and another to start believing everything you hear!

If most of your answers are B, you have the makings of an ex-fundamentalist rebel with neo-orthodox leanings. Unfortunately, your commodity value is low, since the market is glutted with such types right now.

If most of your answers are C, you have obviously gleaned very little of use from this book. Unless you want to be forever known as a kindly but bumbling liberal you had better go back and read it again.

A Christian's Vocabulary
from A to X

A

ADAM: Original sinner but not really his fault. If it hadn't been for the Woman, he might still be tending his garden.

ADMINISTRATOR, fine: Six months after he comes, 93% of the congregation has pledged for the Building Fund.

AFFECTATION: Dressing up for church, not dressing up for church. Carrying a Bible to church, not carrying a Bible to church. Using "Thou" in spoken prayer, using "You" in spoken prayer. Belief is sometimes considered an affectation. So is doubt.

Affectation

AGNOSTIC: *See* Atheist.

AKIMBO: Gesture learned in some homiletics courses. Effective in surplice or academic gown, but in business suit, shows lack of humility.

Alcohol: "If only Americans spent as much on religion as they do on *alcohol* . . ."

Anathema: Right doctrine in wrong church or wrong doctrine in right church. Ecumenism will do away with it.

Apathy: No cause ever found for it, since the clergy is against it and so are the laymen.

Apologetics: Does not mean making excuses for Christianity, but who knows what it does mean? Leave it to the theologians.

Apostles: Only 12 apostles: disciples are something different. How quickly one can name The Twelve divulges something about one's spiritual development.

Art, modern: All decadent. Consists of childish blobs or soupcans. "The product of fallen man."

Artist: A person who paints realistic biblical scenes or who does lovely sunsets in chalk is an *artist*. All others in the arts are egotistical exhibitionists, and enemies of the Church.

Atheist: *See* Agnostic.

Artist

B

Baptists: Sometimes frighten other Protestants by the number of Bible verses they know and the gusto with which they sing.

Bar: The piece attached to attendance pin for two or more years of perfect attendance.

BARTH, BONHOEFFER, BRUNNER, BULTMANN: File in one lump in mental storage cabinet for use in intellectual discussions. Ex.: "As Barth said—or was it Brunner . . ."

BIBLE READING: Five verses in the morning mean a fair day ahead. A whole chapter before breakfast means everything will go right.

BLESSING: Christians are not at all interested in material *blessing*.

BLIND: In some circles, all unbelievers must be considered blind—there is no use in even trying to get them to see.

Bible Reading

BROTHER: All believers are brothers. There may be family fights, but their love always shows through.

C

CHOIR: If suited to no other work, new church members may be relegated to the alto section.

CHURCH DINNER: Together with Strawberry Festivals and Ice Cream Socials, they constitute the most important work of the church.

CHURCH-IN-THE-WORLD: Frightening term no matter who uses it.

CIGARETTE SMOKING: Much more sinful than overeating or careless driving.

CONSTITUENCY: Christians who have money. "We don't want to offend our constituency."

Cigarette Smoking

D

DEDUCTIBLE: Make sure the money you give to church and missions is *tax-deductible*.

DISASTER: A prayer meeting where there is a long pause followed by two people who start to pray at the same time.

E

EPIPHANY: Since we have Christmas from Thankskiving to New Year's Eve, who needs it?

EPISCOPALIANS: Spend the entire service getting up and down. Sing strange and mournful things called "Psalms." All are rich.

EUPHEMISM: In religious discussions, have several handy.

EVANGELICAL: A son of a Fundamentalist.

EVERYDAY CHRISTIANITY: Driving your next-door neighbor to the beauty parlor.

EXEMPLARY CHRISTIAN: Well-bred, prosperous, charming, and handsome individual who never breaks the rules of the established church. Eliminate Francis of Assisi, Blaise Pascal, John Wesley, Martin Luther, St. Paul, Jesus Christ, *et al.*

EXEMPT: Good speakers, well-known Bible teachers, fine singers, and wealthy contributors should be *exempt* from cleaning up after church teas or taking a turn at nursery duty.

F

FALTER (in the way): More genteel than staggering.

FAST: Roman Catholics fast only because the Church tells them to. Liberal Protestants fast only because they need to lose weight. Pentecostals fast only because they are "fanatical." Fundamentalists eat all the time.

FORBEAR: To clench one's teeth.

FOREFATHERS: Bible-believing, Christ-centered Deists.

G

GLUTTONY: One of the "seven deadly sins." Now obsolete.

GOD-IS-DEAD: Just a catch phrase. Nothing to worry about. Laugh gently at little old ladies who ask their pastors if the theologians really mean it.

GODSEND: Unexpected money or suitor.

GRAD: A cute term for young churchmen who have finished college. Often there are special Sunday school classes and conferences for *"Grads."* Such groups must watch out for the infiltration of secretarial school products, the self-educated, and drop-outs.

Godsend

GRAMMAR: "Remember that God loves you and I."

GRUNT: The In way of saying "Amen."

H

HABIT: Always "bad."

HANDICAP: Organ with a broken "F" stop on Easter day.

HANDIWORK: Stuffed animals made from old socks (raising

111

the problem "Shall we charge $1.00 or $1.25?"); potholders in the shape of fish; centerpieces of gilded macaroni and dried beans. God's handiwork is the heavens but unfortunately cannot be sold at the Annual Church Fair.

Handiwork

HATE: Say: "Hate the sin but not the sinner!" Or: "Hate the sinner but not the sin!" Or something.

HEAVEN: Say: "Everybody wants to go there, but nobody wants to die to get there, ha, ha."

HELL: Say: "Each man makes his own hell." Or: "The people who are going to hell wouldn't be happy in heaven anyway." Or: "Hell is still a rather potent myth."—Depending in what company you are.

Hell

HICCUP: Among churchmen, the hiccup is only the result of eating boiled cabbage or drinking coke too quickly. Choir members must follow good hiccup etiquette: (1) Attempt to swallow the "cup" before the "hic" is over. (2) Look compassionately toward the lead soprano as if she did it. (3) Giggle about it with decorum since by now, the entire congregation is looking at you.

112

Hymnal: Bemoan the loss of the "good old hymnbooks" with the "good old hymns." How can they hope to replace "Tell Mother I'll Be There"?

I

I: Word rarely used in the speech of the redeemed.

Immerse: Are you acquainted with the story of the Baptist who was drowned that way? Cite it when occasions arise.

Indignation: Always "righteous."

Indoctrinate: Others do it.

Iniquity: Others have it.

Innocuous: Preaching Hell to people who already believe in it, or Integration to those who already are integrated.

Indignation

Integration: Black and white is not the only kind. Placing a Ph.D. at the same table with a cesspool cleaner, and surrounding the two of them with an op artist, a member of a Fine Old Family, and a teenage hood will integrate the church supper.

Integration

Invective: "Glory be!"

J

JARGON: You will not have arrived as a Christian until you can say five sentences so full of Christian jargon that an unbeliever thinks you're speaking a foreign language. I.e.: "Since I surrendered at Calvary I have a personal quiet time where I break the bread of life each morning. Wouldn't you like to do that too?"

JETSAM: Steeples, paid organists, the woman's auxiliary, hierarchal salaries, deacons, sermons, creeds, faith, the Bible—it depends on where you sit.

Jetsam

JUDGE: Judge Not, but discern to your heart's content.

K

KNEEL, whether to: The most critical decision for a Methodist attending a union service in an Episcopal church.

KNOWLEDGE: Too much of it puffeth one up and maketh him proud.

Kneel

L

Lachrymal: The sight of one's own child garbed in a bathrobe to play Joseph in the Christmas pageant.

Lackluster: The sight of someone else's child garbed in a bathrobe to play Joseph in the Christmas pageant.

Lackluster

Laity: In the opinion of some of the clergy, a necessary evil.

Led: A way to forestall argument or opposition: "I felt definitely *led* to ask you to paint the church/bake all the cookies for next month's meeting/contribute toward the new steeple bell."

Lent: A boon to the religious books market and the tunafish industry.

Legerdemain: Of great use in making "gradual changes" in church policy.

Leprosy: Not so much a disease caused by the *Bacillus leprae* as a beautiful sermon illustration.

Letter: Protestants are always "taking their Letters and leaving" or "Having their Letters sent" from one church to another. But nobody under fifty seems to know quite what a Letter is.

Liberal (church): Place where there is no Wednesday prayer meeting and no Sunday evening service.

Lighten: In certain circles, always used to modify "the load."

Liken: A sermon or Sunday school lesson is never any good unless everything mentioned is *likened* to something else. When preaching to soldiers, liken God to the General; to businessmen, the General Manager. For students, liken Him to a Wise Professor. Bulldozer operators will understand His nature if He is likened to an Omnipresent Contractor.

LOVE: Just mention that there are three different kinds and give the Greek word for each.

Love

LUCKY: Some consider the use of the word the next thing to swearing. Say "fortunate" or "blessed" instead.

LUTHERANS: All Germans.

M

MAGI: The Wise Men. Nobody knows if there were three of them, or if they were really kings. Be sure to mention this during the Christmas Bible class lesson.

MAGNETISM: The best of preachers have it.

MAGNIFICENT: Adjective reserved for cathedrals. Protestant churches may cost as much to build, but never are.

MASTERPIECE: "Praying Hands."

MAUDLIN: Unknown in religious painting or writing. Especially unknown in Christian films.

MENACE: You name it.

METHODISTS: All are middle class, temperate, and given to worry about which ministers will be moved at the next Conference.

MILLENNIUM: A thousand years of peace that theologians like to fight about.

MISSIONARY-LADIES: Single women who know how to traipse

through jungles, paddle canoes upriver, and repair jeeps while wearing skirts. All are camera fiends.

Mitebox: The most moving ceremony of the church year is the children's Mitebox Presentation.

Missionary-Ladies

N

Nickname: "Born-againer."

Nominal (Christian): The supreme insult.

Nonconformist: Prays with his eyes open.

Nonentity: Nonexistent in Christian circles, since every person is invariably considered just as important as Billy Graham or the Archbishop of Canterbury.

Nowadays: Sin has never been so rampant as.

Nourish: Always followed by "the soul."

Nonconformist

O

Offend: Whatever you are going to do, don't. It might *offend* a weaker brother.

OFFERTORY: In Protestantism, refers to "The Lord's Prayer" sung with a high "A" by the bravest soprano available.

OUTLANDISH: Any modern church architecture.

Offertory

P

PACIFIST: Someone who takes the Sermon on the Mount literally.

PENTATEUCH: Say: "Do you suppose Moses really wrote any of it?"

PORTAL: The heavenly word for "door."

PRESBYTERIANS: Once were a dignified people, but now hold services in jazz.

PROFOUND: Preacher who makes up original clichés.

PROPHECY: To set everyone straight say: "It doesn't mean *fore*telling; it only means *forth*-telling." Every preacher who tells his congregation off is really a prophet.

Portal

Q

QUAINT: Any small church that has been redecorated in Early American.

QUARTET: Four grinning seminary students singing "Abide with Me."

Quartet

R

RADIANT (Christians): Their faces emit rays of bright light.

RAFTERS: What a rousing hymn should make ring.

RAIMENT: The heavenly word for "clothes."

RECREATION: A hot game of Scrabble or Rook.

REPROACH: One hasn't arrived until one has *reproached* a fellow believer, preferably in print.

RESPECTABLE: What every churchman should aim to be.

RESTORED: That which has to be done when a Christian stays away from church for more than three weeks.

REVIVAL: Never make fun of the word. Too many others have.

Respectable

S

SABBATH: Day of Rest that for active Christians begins with Sunday school and ends with exhaustion.

SACRIFICE: Donating your best birdcage to the Church Auction

or

Sleeping on the sofa so that four members of a traveling Christian college choir can have your bed.

Sacrifice

SAVED: Never use the word since it is un-chic. Search instead for a clever synonym to explain the need of the human race.

SERMONS: The best of them begin with a joke, continue with three easy-to-remember points and 25 anecdotes, and end with a hasty benediction.

SHELL: Some Christians are always "coming out of shells."

SO-CALLED: The next-to-supreme insult: "A *so-called* Christian."

SUFFER: Some Christians look forward to it. Always "suffer in silence"; then testify at length about the experience.

SUNSET: A picturesque word for "death."

Suffer

T

TABERNACLE: A thing for Sunday school classes to build models of.

TABOOS: Each segment of the Church has its own set, and there is no way to learn them but the hard way.

TALENT: "Use your talent for the Lord"—so long as your talent is singing, playing a musical instrument, preaching, or teaching Sunday school.

TALISMEN: Mustard-seed necklaces, bracelets inscribed with the Ten Commandments, pens inscribed with Bible verses, and expensive Bibles with one's name inscribed in gold on the cover.

TEA: A ritual held in the parish house or, occasionally, the church basement. The women wear hats and the men stand on one foot. No sure escape from the tea exists.

Tea

THANKFULNESS: Do not thank God simply because you feel thankful; thank Him because if you do not, He may not give you anything else.

Tightwad: Person who buys 30¢ worth of cookies at the women's bake sale, or who chips in a quarter toward the minister's Christmas present.

Tithing: To encourage tithing, mention that it will bring prosperity to the tither.

Trumpet: Very popular instrument in some Christian circles, probably because Gabriel plays one. To "use your talent for the Lord," play "Onward Christian Soldiers" on the trumpet.

(*See* Talent.)

Trumpet

U

Ulcer: Shows a lack of trust in God.

Ushers: Two fat *ushers* walking up a thin aisle with full collection plates can cause a calamity.

Ushers

Uttered: What prayers are.

V

VALLEY: Prevalent symbol in religious literature.

VERSION: If you do not own at least five *versions* of the New Testament, consider yourself out-of-it.

Version

W

WEAK (Christian): Another insult. Watch out for this one; it is usually whispered by people who are "strong" Christians.

WINSOME (Christian): A compliment, usually meaning that one is being nauseating about the whole business.

WISHY-WASHY (Christian): Yet another insult, very popular in some circles.

Weak

WITNESSING: Does not mean "buttonholing"—but at present there is quite a debate over what it *does* mean. If in doubt, play it safe, and don't do anything.

X

XMAS: How angry you become at the use of this spelling shows the degree of your dedication.

Xmas

Y-Z

Nothing special leaps to mind beginning with Y or Z. Everyone knows about "yawns," and "zealous" (Christian) is yet another form of compliment. Preparation for Games Christians Play may be considered adequate with a vocabulary extending from A through X.

Format by Morris Karol
Set in Linotype Caledonia
Composed, printed and bound by The Haddon Craftsmen, Inc.
HARPER & ROW, PUBLISHERS, INCORPORATED